WORD GHETTO

POEMS
BY
LORETTA DIANE WALKER

BLUE LIGHT PRESS ◆ 1ST WORLD PUBLISHING

1ST WORLD
PUBLISHING

SAN FRANCISCO ◆ FAIRFIELD ◆ DELHI

WINNER OF THE **2011 BLUE LIGHT BOOK AWARD**
WORD GHETTO

1ST WORLD LIBRARY
809 S. 2nd Street
Fairfield, IA 52556
www.1stworldpublishing.com

BLUE LIGHT PRESS
1563 45th Avenue
San Francisco, California, 94122

BOOK & COVER DESIGN, ILLUSTRATIONS
Melanie Gendron
www.melaniegendron.com

AUTHOR PHOTO
Chris Walker of Walker's Photography
walker9136@sbcglobal.net

FIRST EDITION

LCCN 2011941235

ISBN 9781421886305

*Perhaps the characteristic most central
to the definition of poetry is its unwillingness
to be defined, labeled, or nailed down.*

—Mark Flanagan—

PREFACE

Merriam Webster Dictionary defines ghetto as:
1 : a quarter of a city in which Jews were formerly required to live
2 : a quarter of a city in which members of a minority group live especially because of social, legal, or economic pressure
3 a : an isolated group <a geriatric ghetto> b : a situation that resembles a ghetto especially in conferring inferior status or limiting opportunity <the pink-collar ghetto>

Often, the word "ghetto" usually conjures up negative images, run-down buildings, poverty, property neglect, and imprisonment. Negative connotations such as despair, rejection, and hopelessness are also associated with this word. However; in the confines of any ghetto, there is a wealth of untapped resources, the individuals themselves. This collection is not about a community of people, rather a community of words which cover various aspects of life, both positive and negative. The purpose of this collection is to, if only for an hour, give the word ghetto a positive meaning.

DEDICATION

To my Mama, Mary Walker,

You have been the strength of my existence.
With all the love in me for you,
I wish I could make all of your dreams come true.
Thank you for encouraging me to go after mine.

Special Thanks

I extend much appreciation and gratefulness to my mentor, Diane Frank, for opening up my world with "pushing" and "fifteen possibilities." Your honesty, generosity, and encouragement have exceeded anything I could expect in a mentor. Your insight has helped me to look deeper within myself to discover what truly wants to be shared.

Mary Kay Rummel, thank you for being the magnifying glass and the final editor. Your generosity leaves me speechless.

Also, a note of thanks to Janette Sloper, Alice Greenwood, Ivy Kaminsky, Barbara Nay, and Nancy Clark for rummaging through the pieces and being sounding boards at various times.

I can never say thank you enough to my family and friends. Your support means more to me than I can express. I wish I could find words larger than thank you to convey my gratitude for each of you.

ACKNOWLEDGEMENTS

A thank you to the following publications where some of these poems appeared or are forthcoming:

Big Country Writers: "Pinwheel Predictions"
A Book of the Year, Poetry Society of Texas: "Poetry's Assassination", "Her Words", "Curve of Confusion"
Aries: A Journal of Creative Expression: Texas Wesleyan University: "An Answer to the Question, 'Is That Your Baby's Daddy?'"
Backstreet Publications: "I Have Poetry for Lunch"
Bay Area Writers League: *Texas Writers Conference Anthology:* "Blue Performance"
Big Land, Big Sky, Big Hair (Best of the Texas Poetry Calendar Anthology) "East Texas" (Formerly "It Was")
Borders: *Metro Dallas Home Alliance:* "How I Remember You", "Soaking in Shame"
Calliope: "Blue Performance"
Chaos: "Poet Outside the Box"
Conceit Magazine: "Humming Bird Wings", "Pinwheel Predictions", "Life is Water"
Concho River Review: "Poetry's Assassination"
Encore Prize Poems of NFSPS: "Before Dancing With the Stars"
From Under the Bridges of America: Metro Dallas Home Alliance Anthology: "Abundance", "How I Remember You"
Haltom City Library: "Pinwheel Prediction"
Harp-String Poetry Journal: "A Letter to the Poetry God", "Black History Month Ended Yesterday", "Jalapeño Sun"
Illya's Honey: "When Last I Ate a Cantaloupe"
Legacy: An Anthology of Timless West Texas Writings: "Headlines", "Layers of Memories", "Humility"
Nomad's Choir: "Immortal", "Life is Water"
Northern Stars: "To My Turtle: Sixty Days a Mother", "When I Am Fifty"

Oil And Water: An Anthology of the Permian Basin Poetry Society: "A Letter to the Poetry God", "An Answer to the Question, "Is that Your Baby's Daddy?""

Orbis International Poetry Journal: "The Ancient"

Pennsylvania Prize Poems: "Abundance", "Holes in the Line"

Prayerworks: "Pinwheel Predictions"

River of Earth and Sky: Poems For The 21st Century: "When I Am Fifty"

River Poets Journal: "Hummingbird Wings", "Pinwheel Prediction"

Round Top Poetry Festival Anthology: "Black Feathers"

San Antonio Poetry Fair Anthology: Voices along the River: "The Ancient", "Pinwheel Prediction", "Black Feathers", "Reflections"

Sandstorm Literary Magazine, University of Texas of the Permian Basin: "Poetry's Assassination", "An Answer to the Question, "Is that Your Baby's Daddy?", "Looking for African Essence at Wal-Mart Supercenter", "Defense for a High School English Essay"

Soul Fountain: "Life is Water"

The Sylvan: "I Am"

Texas Poetry Calendar: "Black Feathers", "East Texas" (Formerly "It Was")

Wind, Sand, and Sky: An Anthology of the Permian Basin Poetry Society: "The 8th Street Carwash and Detail Shop"

TABLE OF CONTENTS

VI. BENEATH THE SKY

VII. CAFETERIA CONVERSATIONS

FORWARD

I AM

I am not my dream—a gold princess
with corn silk hair, flower breath and magic hands:

I am color and song
questioning purple melodies
crawling through my swollen fingers
listening to rusty blues chords, I, IV, V
escaping from keys
watching notes lift from the score
become a black blizzard of sound
wanting them to blow—
move me through this storm
of color and song.

THE POEMS

POETRY OUTSIDE THE BOX

A poet stands outside the box,
looking down at ideas bouncing
off bruised walls.
With chin perched on crossed arms,
the poet cries out,
"Hey you down there."
Mystified souls look up,
arms stretched into questions.
The poet points to a far corner,
"Look. I left a ladder for you.
Climb out of your cell."

I

OUTSIDE THE BOX

Word Ghetto

Moonflowers, like some poems, worship darkness.
They open and flourish with white beauty
in the palm of night.
See how they smother themselves
with the moon's pallid smile.
When day is awake in its fullness,
those plants snub the sun
and close like sealed envelopes.

Rejection pricks like their hard porcupine seeds.
It scrapes layers beneath what can't be seen.
I know rejection's pain, the swelling in tender places.
But here I am carving sentences, banishing them
to dwell among other discarded lexicons.

Anger, apple blossoms, white cotton socks,
joy, tears, turbulence
are treated like derelict words.
They are dumped for not fitting
into the suburbia of my shiny polished poem.

I left them abandoned, struggling to survive
where hope is dependent on the economics
of convenience and memory.
I pit them against each other
like angry dogs.
The survivor's bone is my pen.

Does this talk of struggle
and abandonment depress you?
You want a pink smile?
I can't give you one today.

See how the sun flashes its amber teeth
after two days of hard gray rain?
My smile will shine
like that when I find a way to liberate
each rejected syllable breathing
between the pages of my word ghetto.

1

FLUIDITY

Beware if you find yourself dancing
barefoot in the arms of an aged poem.
Those centuries of words
can stampede across the page
and scrape layers from the earth.
They can snag your wrist with mystery
and bruise your stomach with amazement.

They can impede judgment
with the power stashed
inside nouns and verbs,
rescue an ego slipping
into quicksand of self-righteousness,
crawl inside the soul and make you laugh.

Poetry is not delicate.

It is a sturdy target.
Aim arrows of criticism at its big mouth.
They will ricochet against strong teeth.
But its hard hands will not scar flesh,
crush bones, or break wings.
This morning I witness its long fingers
sliding up and down a child's yellow pencil,
joy sweating in its old palm.

OUT OF THE FOG

This morning came galloping
with a hot vengeance
after I had only three hours of sleep.
Oh, to roll time back,
make the hours a black umbrella.

Even the gas pump is impatient.
When I lift the nozzle and insert my card,
it demands, remove card quickly.
Or what? It will not blink its eyes,
hold me hostage in the sun's yellow breath?

How I swell with fatigue, helplessness, anger
under the command of an one-armed soulless dictator.
I squeeze its metal tongue until my tank
and the creases in my palm are full with its salvia—
the smell of someone else's money.

I release after hearing gas spill onto my feet.
The splashing taps me out of my drowsy fog.
It's the same type of fog I found myself falling
into when you asked, "What does the poet mean?"
then answered.

Do not ruin poetry
with that question, coax with your interpretation.
Let your students open a poem
with sticky fingers and find their own way
with gummed words in their hands.

Let them crack it open like a raw egg,
prepare to their tastes,
tell you the rose is a woman.

Once I hurled a smooth stone upwards
and turned before the stone plunged its hard life
back into the earth.

I don't know if it struck, woke
some sleeping desire, startled it into curiosity.
When I looked up,
morning and eggs and stone were the color of air.
I saw only blue dripping from the sky.

DEAR MR. PATTERSON

I'm singing all over this page—Blue Moon right now,
my alto voice straining to reach "D" above middle "C."

Why tell you of my crooning? *Pour cette raison,*
I want you to write me into one of your novels.

I would like to be a singer with a sexy name
like Kitty or Raven. You can make me an object

of desire, contempt, admiration—
sleazy, noble, so wholesome
June Cleaver would require a scarlet letter
in my presence.

Describe my character this way;
say she's a "Dark-haired Beauty,"
with strong legs, swift tongue, tight buttocks,
movements graceful, and lovely like a gazelle.

When she catches the man's eye, watch her strutting,
the way she lifts the curves of her body over his head
as though the air is an elevator.

Her strength feeds his desire, makes him a predator.
He chases her with a pen, scribbles secret words on a tree.

Only you and I know why she sat down
on the dry grass. She wanted him
because he could peel heat from the sun
one sentence at a time.

Defense for a High School English Essay

Seventeen—I protest, "A 'D' still?"
You said, "Do it again." This is again.
The last time was again.
My next again will look like this!
You circle, draw arrows, leave red messages
like *This is not clear.* What's not clear?
I collared those words, wrote them
as though they were created for each other.

I scratched through a few
crowded pages with corrections.
You said rewrite. I rewrote.
I save trees using recycled sheets.

I give you this essay again.
Think this time before you bleed on my words
with your ink. This is my soul you are staining.

POETRY'S ASSASSINATION

Poetry's assassination was not in the newspaper
this morning nor did I see a script of its demise
scrolling at the foot of CNN's news broadcast.
But I was told it is dead as Latin.

Could it have accidentally drowned
in the small lake where poets fish?
Could the media have missed its exhumation?

I doubt if it was suicide.
It would not hang itself with rhythmic phrases
or overdose on syntax or imagery.

I cannot imagine poetry cutting
its soft wrists until the blood of alliteration
drained, leaving it lifeless.

I could not find its multi-faceted face in an obituary anywhere.
Wonder if there is an autopsy on record somewhere,
waiting in a *"to be filed"* box before its official release.

I don't know the origin of this rumor,
but poetry (poetica) is not dead (decessus)!
It lives.
I saw its round belly protruding
through my neighbor's red blouse.
She thinks it is a boy, but it is poetry.

I HAVE POETRY FOR LUNCH

Famine, genocide, war on CNN's plate.
Other television stations prepare a gourmet
meal of who fathered Anna Nichole Smith's daughter?

I opt for variety, select lunch
from a menu opulent with words.

For an appetizer, I sample a Forbes Magazine article
by Mark Stevenson about billionaires with bloated wallets.
The world's third-richest man, Carlos Slim,
is gaining rapidly on Bill Gates and Warren Buffet
with a fortune that grew $19 billion last year . . .

Gates and Buffet share their fortunes, but Slim says,
"Businessmen should not go around like Santa Claus."

For lunch I feast on the poet's tribute to his father,
who taught him to lay bricks, throw stucco and reinforce concrete.

While I eat, CNN flashes images of kids starving in Africa.
Their empty bloated bellies spill into my water glass.

Why choose African children for hunger's face?
When I was a child, mother said, "Eat everything
on your plate. There are starving kids in Africa."

I say now, "There are starving children in America,
Mexico, India and other romantic destinations of the world."

I will be greedy and eat two poems.
I will bloat my belly with words
and write a poem about wealth, then share.

A Letter to the Poetry God
(In Memory of Corporals Scott Gardner, Abel Marquez and Arlie Jones)

I tried to barter with you, Poetry God,
but failed. Now I am reduced to bribery.
I will give you a million poems
if you will give me a word that rhymes with orange.
I do not want a nonsense word for this rhyme,
but a real word that describes the orange pain of grief.

Our city grieves after an evening of insanity
froze a sweltering September day with death.
I could tell you the orange cape of morning
and mourning has wrapped around the city seven
times since it happened.
But I want to show not tell
you of our orange tears of shock and anger.

Confusion is neither mute nor blind.
We know what happened, how it happened,
when it happened, where, why and who.
But you, Poetry God, will hear it again.

A trio of lives was taken away
with blasts of madness.
Their journey began with a quest to aid.
They were fathers, friends, brothers, sons, policemen.
Now their names are engraved in gold
on a plaque that reads *in memory of.*

Every reason the wind gives
as an explanation for their journey's end
is an orange ball of sorrow.
Poetry God, when you give me a word
that rhymes with orange,
I can change the color of grief
and write a poem that will comfort.

IMMORTAL

"Then there was neither Aught nor Nought, no air nor sky beyond.
What covered all? Where rested all? In watery gulf profound?
Nor death was then, nor deathlessness, nor change of night and day.
That One breathed calmly, self-sustained; nought else beyond it lay."
—Rig Veda

I am immortal
a gray ghost traveling through centuries
collector of thoughts and bones
dove and wolf, clocks and dust.

Can't you hear me? Can't you see me?

I am the quiet voice screaming for attention
in sheets of crimson leaves
the innocent folds of a baby's legs
a working girl's cracked nails.

Can't you taste me? Can't you feel me?

I am the ocean's prayer, sequester of souls and words.
My voice sings joy into the gray hymns of sorrow.
I give light its etiquette, the soft cocoon
of space its wide mouth, darkness its dull teeth.

Don't you know me?
I am your poetry—
the pulse, the glue, the eye of society.

For Tom White and Dale Fowler

POET CENSUS

Numbered like centuries of chipped stars,
we stood, waited to be counted, categorized,
divided like sheep and goats
by poetry's crooked staff.

Angelou, Atwood, Oliver were lined
behind Browning, Dickinson, Rossetti,
their mouths fat with words,
tongues thick with gossip.

I leaned closer to hear. They spoke simply
of beauty, love, and how the corners of death
fold us into ourselves and sometimes
it is the wings of poems that lift us back to life.

LETTERS FROM THE EDITORS

Her sad hair drips with this afternoon's downpour,
long limp curls spiral down her face, shoulders, back.
I cannot see her eyes in the gray afternoon,
but see laughter rushing in her arms
when she reaches for the umbrella
and the small hand of a boy—her son perhaps?

How I want to laugh at these letters in my hands,
or send them back—childish?
When I read them, my heart is eight years old
remembering being the last one chosen,
knowing I'm not a choice.
I find the note after recess, blocked with anger:
I didn't wont her. I had two pic her cause coch
say we gotta get everry body.

How I wish rain could cleanse those words
and wash away the hard dry residue of painful rejection
clogging my memory—and these:

Look. We're all writers, too, so we know how it feels.
We're sorry we couldn't use your work . . .

I'm sorry too, I tell the wounded child,
the taste of an envelope's glue fresh on my tongue.

Why I Shall Not Anger a Poem

If a poem can write itself, I shall not anger it.
It may pull me out of bed,
drag my bare feet over Vostok's ice laden land
or through El Azizia's blistering desert sands.
It may try to squeeze me inside the mouth of an atom
or make me disappear in Quaoar's distant cold world.

It may make me a mystery amidst swirls
of covered corrections, a changed mind and mistakes.
Or it may scratch me off the page
as though I never entered the world.

I will approach it with gentleness, play Verdi or Chopin
while it revises, extract words which weigh it down.
Maybe it will place those discarded words in a crystal vase
while they wait for recycling.
They may find themselves in Van Gogh's *Cherry Tree*,
a sonnet, or in the hands of a different poet.

For Teresa Gazella

II

HOLES IN THE LINE

HOLES IN THE LINE

And a pain still throbs in the old, old scars.
—Paul Laurence Dunbar

At the kitchen table I try to unravel the seam
of mystery wrapped around my mother's life.
I pull on the gray thread with casual conversation.
Cotton. I know you picked cotton
when you were young
and dreamed of becoming a nurse
but tell me about your childhood.
She shrugs,
I was born during the depression
and I have been depressed since.
Her answer leaves holes in my history.

I want to know the conductor
who passed this baton of desire
to make words breathe.
She vaguely sketched her life.
Left me to embellish it with questions.

Pain. That's the word she does not use.
It's the hole in the family line
that keeps me from knowing.
Somewhere in the swirling darkness,
there are answers.

I eat my chicken, drink my diet coke,
do not press for any more clues.
When I get home, I hang her strength
from the first branch of the family tree.

UMBRELLA OF SHAME

Flames stampede, red hot hooves
blacken almost two hundred days
of dry West Texas land.

Dead leaves and grass burn
with bovine, houses and dreams.
Manes of gray smoke blow
in an agitated wind.

Prayers for rain and safety soak
ceilings, walls and the long nozzle
of a fireman's hose.
I am safe in this room of poets,
searching for a poem in the cotton fields
of my ancestors' past.

Their stories of sweating and picking
are like incantations,
but they speak nothing of their lives.

My father's breath is in the dust,
his eyes sealed, and my mother
gives me enough words
to leave me burning with suspicions.

Her silence is water outside the womb.
How she protects her children still,
the way she did when we were growing
inside of her.

How I wish she would release those secrets,
make them flames and smoke,
the rotten hard memories of her past, ashes.
Truth will not sear us.
It will cleanse this child of curiosity,

but she holds on to it all.
Her hands are like molten steel,
and secrets continue to rain
on each of us as we walk under
an umbrella of shame.   17

HARVEST MOON

On our way to the Chinese Restaurant,
horns, brakes, tires, chime in with the radio.

Heavy light carpets the night sky.
The moon is impersonating the sun.
Mother says, "We call that a harvest moon.
We used to pick cotton by it."

I try to see her girl cotton hands,
but the little child in me resists.

Nature screwed the lids
off salt and pepper shakers,
let their grains flow together
to create the color of her hair.

Soft lines gather beneath her pecan colored eyes.
There are sister lines like them on her forehead—
barely visible.
Her face does not suggest seventy-six years.

If she stretched her lips slightly,
there would be a half moon
beneath her nose instead of a smile.

I drive, watch her harvest old memories
as I plant a crop of new ones.

JALAPEÑO SUN

There's a handicapped sticker in my glove
compartment along with peppermints,
pens, papers, emergency numbers.
Sometimes the blue plaque hangs
from the rearview mirror like a security badge.
I look through it, watch the future trail
behind while accelerating.

I keep looking back past the rear end
of my car. Beyond a black sedan—
back to my past.
I am a little girl trying to keep up
with my mother's strong muscular legs.

Pomade keeps her thick ebony hair motionless
although her strides are rapid, demanding.
This day the sun had jalapeños for lunch.
Its hot breath burns an extra spicy summer's day.
Her skin shimmers with purpose in the heat.

The ring of sweat on her erect back is a wet target—
my goal. She looks back. I am close behind,
sometimes running in the trail of her steps.

I walk ahead of her now.
I am a scout searching for dangers
she never warned me against,
holes in the streets and uneven sidewalks.

She leans on me for balance,
her strength draining into my shoulders.
I feel the weight of her being a single mother
lifting.

East Texas

It was the fifties. It was the South.
Before my birth, she sought a promised land
not flowing with milk and honey
but rolling tumbleweeds and blowing sand.

East Texas roads were lined with shades
of carrot, amber, scarlet,
trees yielding to the cycle of seasons—
summer to autumn.
Cold had not taken up permanent residence
but made a deposit on the land.

While seasons struggled for position,
her struggles for a new life were forming
along Texas Interstate 20.

Odessa did not welcome her with prestigious jobs.
It was the fifties. It was the South.

She could not eat from their tables
but rubbed crumbs from their pots
and scrubbed their floors for a dollar an hour.

A black woman in the fifties,
in the South, was called girl,
although a woman—
to keep her beneath fair wages, respect.

When I was a girl, she put pride
in a wash bucket, scrubbed it into the floor
for a dollar an hour so the calluses on my hands
would come from gripping a pen.

TWELVE

When she was twelve,
she went shoe shopping in my closet,
chose my white patent leather boots.

She wore them like her own,
took them down paths I never traveled.
I don't know if she walked across shards of glass,
lost coins or corners of disconnected
cardboard boxes as I did.

I came home early, discovered her in my boots.
She was running down the alley trying to beat me home.
She wobbled in them the way we wobble
through our adolescent years.

When I walked through the door,
I did not scold or mention I saw her
racing towards home.
The soles of those white boots blazed with fear.

I let that be her secret.
I had secrets of my own.
That day has rolled into years of memories.

Since then we have shared
shoes, secrets, sorrows, joys,
a life coat worn with complexities
only sisters share.

For Kimberly Walker Schiff

CANDIDATE FOR STATISTICS

He grows up black,
fatherless, poor
candidate for statistics.

Thirteen he cooks,
irons, rolls responsibilities
in a red rubber band, works
for the things we need.

His voice ripens to a
deep baritone.
He sings,
catches passes, runs
swiftly as a cheetah
candidate for a scholarship.

He can balance a world
of black and white,
peel disappointment
from skinned knees,
pray when others curse
his choices.

He grows
into the competent black man
statistics said he could not be,
the father he wished he had.
I sing his praises.
He is each of my brothers.

For Raymond, James, Chris and Vincent Walker

UNSCRAMBLING LOVE

When I lived on Carver Street,
I chalked the sidewalk to play hopscotch,
scratched jacks on the porch.

I learned girl language and boy language,
negotiated deals with my brothers—
a game of marbles in exchange
for making mud pies.

I skipped rope across the grass, chanted:
Cinderella dressed in yella went up
stairs to kiss her fella,
made a mistake, kissed a snake.
how many doctors did it take?

It took at least thirty to cure my misguided kiss.
It took death for us, woman and child,
to sit crossed-legged on the floor.

We undressed, redressed a Cinderella paper doll,
created art on an Etch-a-sketch, used Play-Doh
to build a child kingdom where life ricocheted
off the tower of an emerald streaked castle.

It took six months to learn mother language.
I did not master the syntax of letting go.
There was no bartering with destiny; she is gone.

I play Scrabble now. In my last game,
it took "v" on the blue triple letter square
to get thirty points for love.

To My Turtle: Sixty Days a Mother

You call me Aunt Diamond. I call you Turtle.
You are three. I am forty-eight and childless
until you rolled your pink suitcase into my life.

Your stay temporary—
you, an extra valve in my heart.
Nothing temporary about your dimples deeper
than caverns, your needs urgent as black ice.

They become part of me like the powdered cheese
we mixed in puffy pale macaroni after it cooked.
You stood beside me on your tip-toes, stretched
until your finger is like an arrow pointed at start.
We make our first meal and caramel memories.

You make a zoo of my bathtub with sponge animals.
Paper stickers on the coffee table
and handprints on the bathroom mirror
are transitional phrases in a language
of *I* and *my*. Now it's *our* and *we*.
"I have to do our laundry," and "We have to eat now."
I am not used to those prepositions.

You teach me to eat red Jell-o with my fingers.
Yellow school buses are magical motor gods,
but trucks are more godlike than buses.
They demand more adulation as your pitch screeches
higher when you say, "Look! A truck!"
"Another one!"

Trucks and my love multiply like veins
in a fractured window.
Evening inches its way through the girl lipstick
we put on this morning.

I comb my hair and through layers of feelings,
remember the first night you came to stay with me.

You crawled in my lap. Your pint-sized hand wiped my tears.
You said, "Aunt Diamond, don't cry."
I won't until I see you roll your pink suitcase towards home.

For Turtle (Kanazeya Williams), You helped me grow up.

I Will Take You Tomorrow

Spring is heavy with heat.
Rush hour traffic moves
through lanes paved with chewed gum.

The knots in my shoulders feel like rocks.
I am too tired to go gaiting around the duck pond with you.

I will take you tomorrow and answer all of your questions
while I hold your small hand in mine.

We can swing them like dangling participles.
You seem to like this.

I will not correct your grammar of joy
if this is the way you want to express it,
but I have to sleep now.

My eyes get heavier sooner
and my feet ache more after walking
the path of living fifty years.

During my blossoming life, I've walked hard
over shallow depressions
but softly around assemblies of bees.

Your questioning eyes remind me you are three.
You do not understand these metaphors.

I will explain them to you when you are older, maybe.
I will also explain why this dandelion is not really a flower
but a weed and you can pick it, but that daisy is a flower
and you cannot.
It does not belong to me—neither do you.

Life, death picked both of us from our gardens
and thrust us onto this petal of perplexity.
We have grown together
rooted in the same soil of sadness.

BREAKING THE ICE

We cannot speak of him— the weather remains a safe topic,
fills empty beats of silence so we don't have to reveal ourselves.

Winter's early morning light drips
from the bare branches
of a chinaberry tree.

Streamers of toilet paper are interlopers
in my neighbor's yard,
waving where leaves normally shake
under the winds nervous hands.

Some child thought this prank funny.
Maybe fate smiled at us, too?
The way she brought us together.

The church where we gather has a gloomy face.
Neither light nor trees can change its disposition.
Perhaps the black hearse parked outside
high jacked its joy.

Linked by blood and shock,
we meet for the first time.
Grief clogs the air while we look for him
in each others faces.
Our names are listed like royalty in the obituary,
written as though we grew together.

Outside bewilderment dancing around us,
choreographed by betrayal.
My friend leads me by the arm like a wounded puppy
and gives a voice to the mystery.
She says my name, introduces you as my sister.
We exchange greetings
with the finesse of polite strangers.

Silence keeps a steady beat on our tongues
while we hold each other with our eyes.
This is the only comfort we have to offer
one another while our father lays in his coffin.
The answers to our unasked questions are sealed
in his cold mouth.   *For Bobbie, Mary Ann and Nelson Moore*

SWEEPERS

We are cultured pearls—a necklace of blood and choice.

Laughter rains from us as we sit beneath
the green umbrella watching Bob
sweep the patio table with a wet cloth.

"You missed a spot,"
Mae says with an empty expression.
How many seasons have communed
in this backyard, gifting dirt and leaves?

For thirty seven years,
they have been shining light
between cracks and small places
only the two of them can see.

I don't know this kind of coupling.
I do know a broom
can sweep away a decade of dust
and teach a lonely teenage girl how to dance.

She holds the broom by its skinny long leg
and makes its straw foot sway.
Oh, to see arms and hips, leg and foot
swinging from side-to-side like a pendulum.
She and her green wooden lover stir joy
as they waltz then glide into a samba.

Now I see her on knees pouring a liquid cleanser.
She does not use abrasives.
They leave grit on porcelain and dreams.
I leave her dreaming in a wide white bathtub
with lilies growing in the bottom.

My mind returns to the edge of the Pacific
where the fog is a gray bird lifting
its soft wet wings.
I smell tangerines and oranges growing
in the backyard where Bob and Mae's
dusty millers look like a white flower island.

My garden is fresh; dusty millers, zinnias,
and marigolds are scattered like hope
and these newly found relations.
We are all growing while sweeping away the past,
wiping clean the old dust of our father's sins,
filling the cracks in our souls with love, light—now.

For Bob, Mae Levin and Jerry Moore

An Answer To The Question "Is That Your Baby's Daddy?"

How can a man walk away, with no regards, from a soul that came from his loins, leave it on the side of the world, vulnerable to hard unforgiving blows and drink the accolades of being called a "good man?"

The words blare from the car radio, *"Is that your baby's daddy?"* My mother would say the pink ball of love conceived me. I would add the jagged edges of rejection cut the cord and Mama bled for me. She hung a picture of Christ on the wall and said He bled for me, too. He still hangs there with his thorny crown. When I grow up; I ask the picture why he doesn't care. Do I cry?

Age twelve. My daddy drives up in a silver Grand Prix with his new wife, leaves me walking with the desert heat of Odessa as my companion. The heat of summer's sun is cooler than the pain of rejection that burns inside me as I watch them roll away in their air-conditioned car. I don't cry.

Age twenty. I ask the picture why my daddy sifts through his worn black cow-hide wallet past 10's and 20's to a one time offering of $5.00 saying, "This is the best I can do." I need $12.00 for a bus ticket. I catch an air-conditioned Greyhound and a case of diminished worth. I don't cry.

I ask the picture why Daddy never sends me a birthday card or telephone call or attention, but leaps over church pews to hand the preacher a glass of water. They say he is a good God-fearing man. And the pastor says in his sermon, "Your heavenly father loves you more than your earthly father." This doesn't comfort 'cause this baby's daddy moves heaven and earth not to be a part of my life.

I watch him usher people through the church's double doors in their fine Sunday fancies. He smiles, shakes their hands, leads them down the aisles of righteousness where Christ hangs on the church wall.

30

Once, while in college, death came to visit me. Mom says I look like him—death. He propped himself up on one elbow, leaned over and flirted with me like a teenage boy oozing hormones. I ask the picture, "Why don't you let death kiss me, move his lips over mine and swallow me in its gray passion." I want to cry.

Daddy comes when my eyes are sunken, face drawn, an empty used trash bag. I look at him through death's foggy shadow; see brown eyes that mirror mine and the mold from which I received my hands. A clueless voice echoes in my ears, "Does your Mama still make that good peach cobbler?" He doesn't ask how I am. I don't tell him the cobbler gets better each time she bakes. I close my eyes in pain; remain silent like the picture of Christ hanging on the wall.

Not That Little Girl

You must do the thing you think you cannot do.
—Eleanor Roosevelt

Your photo albums speak when words
are too frail to share memories.
Once you said, "I prayed for a girl, but I got you."
Mama, sorry I was not that little girl.

I liked your sons' Hot Wheels, cat-eyed marbles.
Shunned bows, matching socks,
rick-racked gingham dresses and pink.

How you labored with my hair,
tried to make me look like a princess,
engrained in me, "Ladies sit with their legs crossed
and speak softly."

My body is a billboard of what you did not pray for,
"tomboy" is written on my scarred legs and bruised back.
How lovely were trees, especially the oak in our backyard
on Carver street. It still has my secrets growing in its old limbs.

I rode the poles of our clothesline like steel horses
and galloped beyond places where my dreams could not take me.
I did not chew my food slowly, hurrying to conquer
demons I am still fighting.

How sacred are prayers and to have one
not conform to your desires? Well . . .
Look at me now in my black pumps and pearls,
lipstick and cashmere. Oh, these frills, Mama,
are not your little girl either.

I am sorry for the tea parties I did not have,
dolls I would not dress, grandchildren I will not give you.
I have the red dress you gave me hanging in the closet.
It still holds your shape.

Do you not remember how I was born?
The umbilical cord that connected us
was not made of flesh but strength.
When the midwife clipped it, you said, survive.

III

SWIMMING IN THE DESERT

SWIMMING IN THE DESERT

When the fog of sleep lifted from her eyes,
light was raining down,
pooling outside the window.

She missed dawn's ritual, peeling away
layers of night—exposing hues
hidden behind a wall of darkness.

The sky was pulsating with hope
when she threw back the covers.

Anxiety flooded her as she raced to the kitchen.
She sipped orange juice as the bread
popped up from the toaster like a jack-in-the box.

She hurried bites of dried toast,
buried her head in a drawer as if seeking secrets,
pulled out the same patina swimsuit
she wore yesterday and disappeared
into a sea of jagged white stones.

I don't know who she is.
I see her in my sleep
swimming in the desert,
gathering fists full of dried soil
from an ocean of memories.

GUILT ERADICATION

You can smell the past
—Zahi Hawass

It's hard to live under layers of guilt—
thick as scents of cinnamon and garlic.
I inhale and exhale my mistakes
as though they are who I am, not what I did.

The sour arms of history embrace me
as though I am drowning in my first offense.
They rock me reeking with condemnation
as I perfume myself with good deeds and self-denial.

Who ordered me to pay penitence for the past
by sabotaging my future?
To walk in the present as though absolution
is a golden apple on the forbidden tree?

I've lived half a century, punishing myself
for being ten, nineteen, human.
If I am going to forgive myself,
I must admit first I am not God.

NOTE TO SELF: THANK MR. EASTMAN

If you meet Mr. Eastman
after your life here ends, remember to thank him
for creating the Kodak camera.
Shake his hand before you bombard
him with volumes of photos.

Be specific. Describe each page.
If he seems bored after volume three,
share more later.
Remember—you have eternity
to let him dote over your collection.

Start with the black and white photo
hanging on your mother's bedroom wall.
She garbed you in a frilly dress and matching bonnet
then toted you off to some photography studio.

After fifty years your ten-month old cherub face
is still posed in innocence on her bedroom wall.
Mention this is the only picture of you as an infant.

When you are finished with your promenade
through the past and he witnesses your
first dance,
first crush,
first car,
explain the glossy blank page clutched in your hand
was reserved for the child you never had.

WHAT THE PICTURE DID NOT SAY

Graciousness is more important than a beautiful hairdo . . .
—Charles Perrault

Cinderella and Snow White
are on lunch boxes now.
Their tiaras prick little girls in the fingers
while they write the same dream—
I want to be a princess.

Cindy's worn that same dress
since the sarabande, minuet, gigue.
Little Miss Snow's blood red lips will never chap.
They cannot grow out of their beauty.
History has stunted their growth,

but you, my friend, how your beauty has changed.
Look at you in your red rhinestone cap!
Smile shaped to a warm "O,"
scalp clear as a full moon.

You have no pumpkin, apple—kiss to change cancer.

Even after that word invaded your vocal chords
and left your tongue limp with disbelief,
you found your voice, named the fear.

We pause, pose for the memory I am looking at now.
Laughing over fortune cookies and tea,
speaking of hairless brows, lashless lids, chemotherapy,
your plans for many tomorrows.
You never say words like courage, strength or hope.

I did hear you say, between pass the Sweet 'n' Low
and these rolls are good, *I'm grateful.*

For Anita McDowell

37

LAYERS OF MEMORIES

Dawn dumps the last fragments of darkness
into the sky's blue bowl.
10:00 AM yards of light thread across the window.
By afternoon the sun is a wool trench coat.

A throng of memories sweats from my pores.
This afternoon's violent heat
reminds me of the summer when I was ten.

My two younger brothers and their friends are a mob,
anger boiling like the Sanhedrin's after Stephen's sermon.
A crush of them rushes and drags him out of the city.
Filled with heated indignation,
their hearts are harder than the hissing stones
they use to pelt his body.

I watch the mob corner a horny toad,
a fist of West Texas sun baring down on its spiny back,
horns protruding above the eyes,
eyes wide like spotlights—
its spiked armor futile against their fury.

Armed with jagged desert rocks,
they stone it for crawling across the yard,
for being different, for being weak.

When it is still,
they run and play like victorious warriors.
Their boyhood innocence stained
with red on a handful of stones.

TATTOO CONVENTION

She shows me a picture of a cat,
tail curled into a question mark,
says, "This is what I am going to get."

I find myself walking up and down concrete aisles,
eyes wide with childish amazement and apprehension.
The San Angelo Central High School Mariachi Band
is studded with gold outfits singing Viva la America
at the West Texas Tattoo Convention.

Curiosity lifts my head
to a banner hanging from the ceiling's dark mouth:

We, the tattooed people of Texas
and members of all associated counter cultures,
do solemnly declare our artistic independence
from America, in order to form the Texas Tattoo Nation.

Standing in black curtain booths,
bodies tattooed with roses and hearts,
skeletons and grapes, fire and light—
are canvasses of declared independence.

At the Final Sin station, a woman sits like a statue,
blouse draped around her waist, milky breasts exposed,
nipples concealed with two strips of blue tape
as the artist inks lines and curves.
I see her later, blue wings flying from her chest.

At the door a tattooed couple smiles gloriously
as they show pictures of their virgin skinned infant.
How beautiful is the world when not colored with judgment.
I collect business cards like gifts
from *Th'ink Tank, Hell Bomb, Luar Airam,*
Calixto Pozo, Katja Ramirez Perfection Tattoo,
buy a T-shirt for breast cancer,
walk away from their world.

Creed by Bobby Lynn Shehorn

ABUNDANCE

After seeing Michael Nye's "About Hunger" Exhibition

When life is fissured
like a ripe yellow melon,
and woeful circumstances eat from it
until the soul is a rind of shame,
hunger festers,
becomes a deep brooding wound.

If hunger is darkness, what of light?
Is it like a layer of skin love can put on?
And who can fit such skin,
give a bowl of soup, fist of bread.

I fast to know such darkness.
My tongue is wet with choices.
how can I say,
I know how it feels
to exchange pride for a cookie?

You with begging eyes, cracked skin,
dried mouth, empty hands—
hands now diving in dumpsters, swimming
through a sea of discard,
catching chicken bones—fear.
Forgive me.

I sat down with my full stomach to write
about the sky's generosity last night,
how it opened banks of clouds,
washed the city in relief and when I woke,
my mood rhymed with the color of morning.

I wish my words were seeds.
You could eat them to fill your emptiness.

How I Remember You

I watch winks of sunlight scoff at the sky,
listen to your wide voice
singing into impending darkness.
You sing a subtle melody like jingling coins.

Your soprano a rainbow of joy
over a pot of begonias,
glass of green tea.

The homeless man—the one in the mall
wears a ratty army jacket,
pants a canvas of filth,
feet laden with scabs.

His beard is a pasture of white neglect.
He speaks to the mannequins
with a voice the timbre of bees.

He limps the breadth of the mall
rummaging through steel mouths of vending machines.

When he finds abandoned coins,
they are silver jewels he hordes in his pocket.
I watch him swagger, swing his crutch like a baton
directing your melody towards his next meal.

Soaking In Shame

Since I was old enough to clasp my hands,
fold my body into humbleness,
Mama instructed me to pray.

Now I lay me down to sleep
I pray the Lord my soul to keep
and if I die before I wake,
I pray the Lord my soul to take,

and please let it be dry.

Twelve years old I wake soaking in shame,
sheets stained with a gold ring of insult;
body, mattress, air perfumed with pee.

I'm thirteen before I wake with only scents
of Irish Spring seeping from my skin.

In San Antonio in search of a restaurant,
I count at least thirteen souls
stretched along the sidewalk,
clothes knotted together like cotton fingers,
bodies folded in homelessness.

I wonder if they pray
bedded beneath the sky's black awning,
music, money, gaiety dancing in distant darkness.

For a glassy second a pair of dull eyes dart past us,
and rainbow colored umbrellas line the Riverwalk
in the shiny summer night.

Their faces are shadows
as we walk around them
hugging our purses,
the stench of urine,
tobacco, fear, frustration
spitting at our heels.

Enough

Sunday morning wakes
with a lazy smile and the First Baptist Church
choir singing hymns on channel seven.

I have no sermon for the sun or grapefruit
for the short-nailed, gray-haired, tattered-clothed
woman stocking breakfast? dinner?
from a garbage dumpster
into a Ruby Red Grapefruit box.

I avert my eyes, give her space to shop
without an audience of pity.
I am walking with an I-POD
and empty pockets.
This is all I have to give her—privacy.

I do not know what she will eat tomorrow
or where she will sleep.
I sleep beneath nine hundred square feet,
moan about not having enough space,
long for more.

I am the first to complain of the world's waste,
how we stuff the earth with things
she cannot swallow.

Last night I dined at Logan's Steakhouse,
drank iced tea, ordered too much food
and a to go box.
All of my life's contradictions are sealed
in white Styrofoam,
waiting to be thrown away
while I walk into a second helping of sunlight.

43

DUST AND STONE

You are in your grave,
sheltered from the debris of pain
you swirled in my life.

I am in the doctor's office,
the air in my lungs, concrete.
My emotions are like five orange marbles.
Sadness and anger thriving like weeds.
If there is a prayer for this,
I am praying the wrong prayer.

Betrayal is in the syringe
stinging with every jab of the needle.
Grief does not make me sick,
it's their secrets.

Well, Doc, I have a red secret,
scarlet as maple leaves,
more crimson than the Cone Nebula,
ruby like Dorothy's slippers.
It's a flame on my tongue,
the cherry I will not allow them to pick.

If my secret is poisonous, I shall die.
I will not tell it to them—
but of dying I will say this
Death is part of life. Life is a straight razor.

I want to use it to amputate, decapitate, burn death,
destroy this darkness
whose ashes are enough
to keep it among the living
until we are dust and stone.

ODE TO A TENNIS SHOE

A pair of old worn brown gym shoes
dangle from a telephone wire
at the intersection of Tanglewood and 42nd Streets.
Laces knotted together with mystery,
thrown up like a cup of cooked wheat pasta,
left hanging.

They are two snooping soles eavesdropping
on a flock of blackbirds flying south
through a day too old and tired to think
about a hesitant green tongue sticking
out through the earth's half cracked smile.
If she'd open her mouth, yawned even,
the stars could drag it into tomorrow
by way of Orion, Draco, Hercules,
past a dense patch of gray clouds
above two cows grazing in a pasture
across from a sign that reads Pavement Ends.

Its passion is like a splinter
lodged deeply in the skin,
and desire is like a pair of tweezers.
The pain of not having what lies beneath
is more excruciating than the probing.
When it bleeds with freedom,
I scratch my hand, feel the flesh
around another splinter swelling.

PERSISTENCE OF MEMORY

Nothing happens . . . but first a dream
—Carl Sandburg

I say this of dreams—
it's criminal to chain, squeeze them into bottles,
cage them like animals.
They will grow spikes like vines,
poke holes, escape like Houdini.

When you close your eyes, they appear
 in the soft flesh of a tomato, the kimono of a geisha doll,
seeds of a pomegranate,
and when you open them, they will walk without feet,
climb without arms, sing without voices
on the white cusp between waking and sleeping
even if you forget them.

I am awake, looking through silvery breath
at squash, apple, pumpkin-colored
mountain tops and roads— a banquet of beauty.
I did not know how to dream of New England in the fall.
I know the flaming eye of a Texas desert sky
blinking heat and lust,
its landscape crammed with clear wide space,
but this chilly blue air is a brocaded silk hat.

I wear it while I stare at a branch
of leaves in the middle of a maple tree.
It's limp, a dangling crimson cocktail glove.
See how fancy it is flopped over a leafy ocher skirt.
Oh, if only that maple had pearls!
If only I could fly it back to the desert.
If only I could wear it like a ruby memory.

JEALOUSY BURNING

She's a goddess sitting cross-legged
on a beige folding chair.
Snug jeans reveal tight muscles and perfect curves.

Long brunette hair drapes her slender shoulders.
Sun painted skin highlights hazel eyes
fixed in the direction of nowhere.

My legs are scarred, darkened
where life rubbed them together.
Age replaces youthful muscles.
Gray is spinning webs in my hair,
and gravity weighs heavy on my shoulders.

I see her before she sees me.
My envy wraps around her thin wrist
like strings wound around the pegs of a guitar.
Our gazes collide in the middle of the room.
My only choice is to force a smile.
She nods and exposes straight ivory teeth.

I say under my breath, "If only I had her beauty."
Silly soul, who will cry if you disappear
into the darkness of another's shadow?
Try to sing soprano with their alto voice
stuff your size ten's in their seven's?

The sky does not desire to dance
like the ocean, nor the cardinal to mimic the lark.
How small to wish for another's voice,
long to grow in their skin.

Rationale flees like grass stampeding
across a desert plain.

We are both wearing the same brand
of black suede boots.
Envy crowds my closet.

Next garage sale I stick a five dollar
price tag on the shoebox—watch the new
owner walk away with her bargain
wondering if she will feel jealousy burning in those soles?

The Weight of Rage

Distance is God's smile stretched
across the oceans,
and fear is a stake in my thigh.
Tethered to the cross
of someone else's decisions.

Legislature cuts education funding,
their blade slicing through the future.
My blood feels like anxiety
and I bleed with it.

Bleeding until I am no longer flesh,
but old words trapped
in the creases of soiled paper.

Hold the discarded sheets close to your ears,
listen to echoes of betrayal.
Those dark angry words are pleas for security.

They came with abandoned innocence
spilled onto the page like drops of trust.
The weight of their rage
makes my fingers clumsy beneath the pencil.

Tonight I will tuck myself in a boat of hope
and ride the wave of uncertainty into another day.

IV

Scars

I wish the scars of the past remained scars.
However, it seems some soul manages to cut the bruises,
reopen wounds and start the bleeding all over again.

Hummingbird's Wings

If we could move our souls
to forgiveness
like the hummingbird's wings,
hate would disappear,
evaporate like a morning mist.

STILETTO

The sun is on sabbatical.
Aquarius is wearing its February self
when three white teenage boys
in a white pick-up truck shout
from the window, "—you—."

When I walked into the store, my head was high
as the moon floating in its freedom.
Now, it's hanging limp with anger—disbelief.

I feel the shame my mother did when she was a little girl,
and the mother before her, when hatred was hurled
with such openness and conviction just for being.

And that word they use is as pointed,
not sexy, as a black stiletto.
I refuse to say it.
Use whips, water, ropes or chains—
they've been used before.

I've trained my tongue to make it silent
although I hear it blasting from car CD players,
watch heads bop hypnotically
to its new financial meaning. I remember the old one.

Oh, Ancestors, our brothers spit on your graves
with gold teeth and chains, expensive cars and bling—
use that word to gain fame
and the ones in the pick-up—you knew their type of fury.

I want to move where that word does not exist
but there is nowhere to go.
Ignorance like greed pollutes every artery of air.
I inhaled their hate,
but have decided to exhale forgiveness.

GO BACK TO AFRICA

Interest among the South's black population in African emigration peaked during the1890s, a time when racism reached its peak and the greatest number of lynchings in American history took place . . . Most free blacks simply did not want to go "home" to a place from which they were generations removed. America, not Africa, was their home . . .

You say, *Go back to Africa.*
I've never been to Africa;
neither has my mother,
nor her mother.
But somewhere in this life tree,
a black mother was uprooted,
shipped across an ocean's salty mouth,
singing fear in chains.

Salt-stench stained her hard bed.
The waters that washed her away
from Africa's proud sky
and its earth beneath her nails
could not wash away the smell
of slavery.

My African mother had many sons.
She said, go back home sons,
away from whips and dogs,
cotton and hate, sun and blood.

Your father's father
and the father before him
hung my mother's sons from branches
when they tried to go back
to a place where they had never been.

In the pages of history,
I see their legs hanging
over the place of their birth;
they inherited America, too.

WHIPPED

Some slaves' backs appeared as
"an undistinguishable mass of lumps,
holes and furrows by frequent whippings."
—Thomas Woolrich

The good old days were only good
for those who had the goods.

If your skin is the same color as mine,
you understand the fatigue
of a whipping board—
blamed for things broken and dark,
cursed for your existence.

If you know the crush of spirit,
taste of scorn, feel of hate, color of accusation
before a trial, or an offense occurs,
your ancestors' dignity tethered in chains
and nakedness.

If you despise the name
yoked around your neck
to make you inhuman,
a commodity, an excuse
to destroy in the name of the Lord,

If your great grandfather prayed
Jesus is not blonde
and the cross will not fall from the church flaming,
you know the hymns of struggles,
dance of escape.

If you learned to release the past
without rope burns on your hands—
you understand
what it is to be black,
in America.

BLACK HISTORY MONTH ENDED YESTERDAY

For Brianna, this is what I could not say in class.

When the sun comes back, and the first quail calls,
follow the drinking gourd. For the old man is waiting
for to carry you to freedom
—Follow The Drinking Gourd

February laughs with heavy warmth.
I swim with slow strokes in a pool of cream
and caramel faces with sprinklings
of dark rich chocolate.

Listen. These words are a map.
The song swirls around the classroom,
lifting souls into the melody.

When the sun comes back, and the first quail calls,
follow the drinking gourd. For the old man is waiting
for to carry you to freedom

I parade the book in front of them,
my fingers a map to the title:
Follow the Drinking Gourd.

Children gather at my feet like seeds
dumped from a package.
I read—the characters an androgynous shade of black,
an attempt to sanitize slavery.

We are a rainbow shade of people
my mind roars my mouth, mute.

I flip to a man standing on the auction block.
Arms folded across his loins, head bowed,
muscles rippling waves of strength,
    NEGRO FOR SALE.

Your caramel face colors with recognition.
Eyes fix on the page then dart
around the room searching for a safe way
to tell me, "Negro means black."

"Why is he for sale?"
The seeds are a forest now, tender limbs growing
with curiosity as they wait for my answer.
"Slaves were property like animals."

My words drain expression from your face,
silence settles on us like a gray fog. I read on.

I walk into a red hibiscus with March
blocked beneath it; your eyes following me—still,
your question traveling on my shoulder.

Child, this is what I cannot teach you.
Black History Month ended yesterday,
but not for me.
I am rooted in blackness still fighting the past,
those who blame me, my ancestors
for everything wrong and evil in the world.

Their names for me are not polite.
They want me to go back to a place
where I've never been.
I inherited America, too.

ONE HUNDRED SIXTY-NINE PANCAKES LATER

And then they all sat down to supper. And Black Mumbo ate twenty-seven pancakes, and Black Jumbo ate fifty-five, but Little Black Sambo ate a hundred and sixty-nine, because he was so hungry.
—Helen Bannerman, *The Story of Little Black Sambo*

One hundred sixty-nine pancakes later
I am stuffed with history.
Prejudice is sticky on the tongue,
oozing tiger butter on Sambo's pancakes.

A peoples' dignity slain, not with sword and gun,
but with chains choked until freedom drains invisible.
My ancestors'anguish filled cotton purses,
helped build a nation who thought them less,
and in the Mississippi muddied feet were bound
by the South's deep hatred of their black soles.

And I say to the Mississippi:

If you call me a thief, base your accusations
on my determination to sneak, crawl
through cracks of racial injustices
not because I'm black

If you call me ignorant, make sure it's
because I kept going under adverse circumstances,
chose not to quit when odds were against me
not because I'm black.

If you weigh the past with forgiveness,
you will hear the husky voice of hatred slip
on your crimson-stained floor, and

If you hear me whistle hallelujah instead of "Dixie,"
it's because I'm black.

I Loved a White Man

and he loved me.
Now he has a white wife
and white children.
I have poems about being black,
a green garden,
a ghost of regret.

He said, "Come with me,"
but I was not strong enough to fight
a world that told me I was free
but not free to love him.

The old ways frowned at us,
their beliefs a slow wedge.

But we laughed
even after a crack head
said, "I hope you have a lot
of black and white zebra babies."

We laughed
after sideway stares.

We laughed
because with change,
promises of change,
there are things that cannot change—

he in his whiteness,
me in my blackness.

Looking for African Essence at Walmart Supercenter

Walmart's parking lot is an obstacle course.
Silver baskets are strewn from end to end.

Inside I search for African Essence, *an herbal blend*
of maximum revitalization and ice.
My search leads me past the magazine racks. On the cover,
"Beauty experts reveal celebrity secrets and how
you can look like them. See page ninety-four."
My African Essence is neither on the page nor the shelf.
I change my focus. This time I search for "AA" batteries.

In the electronics department a shrill voice solicits
the cost of a tag-less television.
"I have a fifteen-year old nineteen inch Magnavox.
I got it for $50.00 at a garage sale. It's pretty scratched
up on the top. The picture is good though. The remote
control is gone. Lost or something. That's what
I'm really looking for, but how much is this T.V.?"

They shuffle through price tags while I rummage through
a half empty shopping basket, avoiding their eyes, pretending
I am not listening, but I hear how life changes course,
sends us in a direction we did not dream
when we greeted a white morning.
I believe the world stocks all my desires, needs,
but I haven't found what I'm looking for—find
myself a voyeur like the electronic eye
monitoring me while I search.
I want to stand in the middle of the aisles, hold up a sign
that reads: "Help me find African Essence."

MOTH BALLS BENEATH MY FEET

From the air
they are a maze of dirty
strings weaving in, out
among themselves.
On the ground
they are roads, webs
of decisions.
I travel only a few.

They are artificial stars,
watts of strategically
placed impersonators.
On the ground
they are lights,
white balls of security
limited by distance.

I look down on a world
that said a poor black girl like me
would never go anywhere.

Possibility spreads her
infinite fingers, points
in the direction of you can.

Here I am, sitting
on a throne of choices—
the world's negative predictions
moth balls beneath my feet.

V

SHADES OF LOVE

PIETY

Tenderness is the heel prints cast in my memory
where stars waltzed across my stomach after touch.

I tried to explain this to you.
I will keep your name a secret
when answering your question.
I will answer on paper only
with today's damp air and bloated sky—
rain coming and going gently as my witnesses.

It is not out of piety or shame that I do not write of sex,
for it is not only sacred, but frightening,
a hard smooth snake stalking in darkness,
a bargaining chip on the raggedy corner of Second Street,
an advertisement campaign for the Super Bowl,
the last option for a box of Cornflakes and Oscar Meyer bologna.

It is a weapon against little girls and naive women—
their voices squeaking with guilt on a therapist couch,
a thorn poking at a single mother's responsibilities,
an obsession that will strip a woman down
until she is left with only a pair of crimson stilettos
bending her desperate back.

It is powerful enough to change history, build empires,
destroy families, create a child,
and even in its loving, laughing, wonderful beauty,
I will not paint its portrait on erotica's lust colored canvas.

Before Dancing with the Stars

I am not sure when it happened.
Maybe before morning became a pair of binoculars
or when darkness grew arms and legs,
swam to the other side of the world.
Australia? China?
I was asleep.

I do know in my dream
I opted not to dance the tango
but chose a waltz instead.

I waltzed with wind, pink begonias,
a corndog in my hand.
I don't like corndogs as a rule
but the children's laughter made me crave one.

My fingers covered with mustard
as I waltzed with an ice colored
smile on my face.

I smiled when my pencil became a flamenco dancer,
   maracas, metaphors
   claves, couplets
   the marímbula, meter
   drums, a dramatic monologue.

Words gyrated on my eyelids
while Ricky Ricardo and Lucille Ball
danced cheek-to-cheek at the Copacabana.

When I wake, I will buy a yellow boa
and learn to dance the rumba.

For Jackie Woods

Her Words

Your love was a solid mountain, not a hope or a guess.
—Naomi Shihab Nye

When we met, I thrust a Polaroid
in the hands of a nearby conventioneer.
We posed, smiled larger than a first meeting.
The shutter on the camera's eye winked.
We were bound eternally by light. I have the only copy
of our faces framed in a four by six space.

You tasted a cup full of my words,
said you liked the flavor of my voice.
I tasted your words, became gluttonous,
filled myself with pages and pages of them.
I liked the feel of your voice.

I have carried your words with me
in airports, the doctor's office, post office
grocery store, automobile repair shop,
and the drive-through window at Dairy Queen.
They have sat in my classroom, soft on my desk—a refuge
between classes of children singing into their futures.

We exchanged words through thin lines.
The last time you wrote you called me friend.
My eyes hung onto that word—friend
held it like I hold memories.

You told me you lost your father this year.
I search for his name, find it and your words:
Your love was a solid mountain, not a hope or a guess.
With those words, I saw the greatness of a man I never met.

I told you I had losses this year, too.
Sadness followed me from February to December.
When you wrote friend, I added your loss to mine
then wrote words to comfort, made them a tourniquet,
tied it around a year that bled grief.

For Naomi Nye

64

WHEN I AM FIFTY CREED

In the year two thousand eight, I will be fifty.
I will not hide behind twenty-nine and holding.
I will release that part of my life with white balloons.

January I will make this announcement:
I will be fifty this year.
After September six, I will say *I am fifty.*

I will let gray blossom
in the garden of my black hair,
tell waitresses to call me woman, not girl.

I will ride a bike, feed ducks,
live a rainbow life
reciting centuries of traditions
although a half century old.

I will write my own birthday card,
the wrinkles in my hands—the envelope.
The card will read:

"I left a trail of flowers on my way up the hill.
Pick as many as you like,
but leave the pansies for me."

For Carol and Barbara Hall

CURVE OF CONFUSION

The disease holds her secrets captive—
memories of her first dance, love,
time we first met.

We eat, she smiles, discovering
the world for the first time—again.
Diners suspect nothing.
We know her smile is a curve of confusion—
search for words to wake her memory,
but they are clumsy feet slogging
through Alzheimer's fat dark tangles.

We speak of when the three of us
     frequented dollar movies,
     ate Mexican food at Casa Ole,
     took a road trip to McKittrick Canyon.

She smiles again, eyes staring into a universe
neither of us can understand,
says my name once before disappearing
into a gray cocoon of forgetfulness.

Silence dances. Our hands are kites,
the two of us drive away waving,
knowing her memory is like the sound
of loose gravel gripping our tires.

For Vonnie Walker and In Memory of Joan Marchbanks

ANONYMOUS

The first time I see you
is from a hard plastic seat,
far left section, middle row of the gym.

Before the game starts, I watch you pace
the length of fifteen neatly lined chairs—
the soles of your brown shoes tapping
up and down the thick boundary line.

After the first quarter
I learn your routine—
walk, squat, stand, stuff hands in pockets,
the soft lining collecting your anxiety.

The whistle blows,
the team scampers, huddles
around you like a laurel wreath.
I watch your mouth move
but can not make out the words.

They rush to the court, hope bouncing in their feet,
your passion scuffing the hardwood floor.
I watch you begin another cycle:
pace, bend, sit, stand, shout, clutch fists.

The whistle blows this time
with less than ten seconds remaining on the shot clock.
My heart leaps at you, for you, for them.

When the final shot of hard rubber rips
through the web of string,
and the buzzer beeps,
and the crowd's cheers cover the gym,
and the scoreboard flashes eighty-one to eighty,
the hard plastic seat is a cannon.
I shoot to my feet, explode into fragments
of shock, disbelief, ecstasy.

You stroke your hair in victory,
shake the other coach's hand.
I remain anonymous.

GIRL WONDERING

Plants thrive off of the carbon dioxide
we give to them when we talk.
—Anon

Silence is the only way I can look at this.
I shall not say what it is
or it will become true again,
and I have spent many years making it not so.

But the little girl I left burdened
with it screams at me, "You, too!"
Oh, brown-skinned child,
gray hair does not make you strong.
It makes you a master of secrets
like the light riding on dawn's pink back.
It does not share the night's dark and fearful stories.

Let's leave our stories buried.
See my neighbor, how she pulls weeds,
gathers twigs, waters her geraniums,
speaks to them, showers them with soft music.
She does not disturb earthworms
hiding in the red wet dirt;
that's why her flower garden is beautiful.

Do not envy the tenderness she gives.
I will play you soft music, too—
Bach, Beethoven, Braxton,
but I will leave silk flowers in the window.
Their leaves will not brown, wither, fall—
like the ivy on my kitchen table
dying from silence.

A History Lesson on the Oak Tree

Mighty oaks from little acorns.
The broad trunk is a brace for their backs.
Their bodies touch; they feel the heat of silence,
inhale, exhale distance; rooted like melted snow.
She's leaving—wants to grow.

Amputated oak leaves are a wall.
He picks one up, examines it for answers—
hopes its gold fingers will spin words.

Fall pears and oak leaves
make wonderful promises.
Pile them in with oranges and other bright
fruit and desire colors the air.

She is the center of his world.
The oak is a symbol of strength
and endurance, the national tree of England.
He interrupts, voice fragile as a dried leaf.

We're not in England.
In Celtic mythology, the oak is the tree of doors,
a gateway between worlds,
a place where portals can be erected.

He stares into the world she desires—devoid of him.

The leaf falls, echoes in his rushed tracks.
You met someone new?
You were supposed to fight for me!

She stains the trunk with tear and blood—
a broken blade buried beneath dead leaves,
along with their history.

HANDCRAFTED

In the pale husk of her room,
she sits in a maple rocking chair,
handcrafts an apron, stitches secret messages
and her mother's wisdom in each seam,
craggy hands moving like fleshy wings—

sewing as a plastic mouthed girl watches her
from a dusty shelf.
She has no mother or pink ribbons for her hair,
gingham dress tattered, frayed with tears,
stained with years of handling.

She'll wash the little girl's feet, too—
thinks that is holy—to wash feet,
bake sweet bread with hot butter,
eat chocolates from gold wrappers.

Her hands are still now.
She sits listening to memories,
hears whispering in the needle—
his name for her.
Not April or Violet, May or Rose,
June or Jasmine, he calls her Unstable.
She rocks with that name pricking her back.

IRONY

Time broke all of Emily Post's rules.
She chewed with her mouth wide open,
showed all of her teeth biting mystery,
wiped it on her sleeve
smearing the past and present.

She propped heavy elbows on the table
then shook space and air.
Look what she did with all that shaking.
Tonight's darkness is thicker than tar
and stars crowd the sky
like spectators at The World Cup.

Last week I strolled through the neighborhood,
watched a bouquet of balloons
float across a dawn streaked sky.

They looked like helium filled lollipops
with apple green, butterscotch, bubble gum
colored heads drifting into a medallion of fading light,
their tails wagging like happy puppies.

I walked rejoicing the only pain
my body knows is arthritic knees and hands.
Also thinking about what you wrote.
"The chemo went well. When you see me,
try not to be shocked."
How I want to tell you—
save your fear for graver things.

This morning we look at each other
in the mirror while I wrap your scalp
with a red, white, and blue scarf.
We smile while you turn from side-to-side,
making sure nothing shows. 71

Before drifting in and out of sleep
last night, I did stare at you— not out of pity.
It was because both our heads were covered
with bandanas. Mine was braided
in intricate patterns,
woven together like a maze of corn.

Yours was smooth like a pink balloon,
with its tail wagging like a quiet warrior.

In memory of Joyce Sandra Uhlir

THE ANCIENT

All people dream, but not equally.
Those who dream by night in the dusty recesses of their mind,
wake in the morning to find that it was vanity.
But the dreamers of the day are dangerous people,
For they dream their dreams with open eyes,
And make them come true.
—D. H. Lawrence

Fingers of light peel my eyes open,
draw back the curtain of sleep.

An Ancient—pale, brilliant
crouches between earth and sky,
a coffin of words at his feet.

Luminous hands drum
the rough pine box,
his voice, soft like blue, chants:
These are the words you fear,
have not spoken, wished you knew.

He lights three lavender candles, opens the coffin, ascends.
Words—love, hope, success spill from his heel print.

I scrape at them, knuckles raw with chase,
brows moist with determination.

Ancient gathers three laurels,
crafts a wreath, places it on my head.
Sing your name until you are your name.

We dance, the wreath light on my head,
his heels heavy on my feet.

ANATOMY OF THUNDER

Ask a child to say
the last three letters of Happy—slowly.
P-P-Y.
Listen for innocent laughter
and the mischief in little boy humor.
P-P-Y he will say again, watching
for your response.

What can make today's sky smile?
See how pitifully lonely it looks,
the sun snubbed by those elitist rain clouds.
They must have spent all day piling
water in their gray bouffant heads.

Just look at them hovering like buzzards,
basking in this desert city's obsession.
How it fusses over their presence.

They pose like a star I know.
Shall I tell them we were not created
to be worshiped?
The soul is too small
to contain such adoration;
it will fall under the weight
of its own self-importance.

Turn away from the sky.
Look at the hundreds of blackbirds
in that naked tree! They are hieroglyphics,
tell of winter's cold expression.

It grew weary waiting on fall
to finish loosing its auburn hair.
Day after day soft leaves fell.
The wind collected the brittle locks,
made a wig the bald maple cannot wear.

74

Room 2525

Who will sleep where my dreams are cold—
smoothed on fresh cotton linens?

The silver-haired man in creased khakis,
burgundy winged-tip shoes, and crisp white button down?

The sandal-toed couple in matching Hawaiian shirts?
Their tanned smile reeking newlyweds,
or the lavender perfumed woman
clutching her Macy's sack like a prize?

Will lovers rendezvous knowing
their promises are lies they tell themselves,
and each other to make it through the weekend?

Will any of them look out the window
at dawn, see the Gateway Arch is an eyelid
over the sun's pink eye?

And what of the red-capped man in Kiener Plaza
collecting garbage in the city's sleepy haze,
early morning slumping on his shoulders?

With slow even strides, he pushes a gray trashcan
past a platoon of taxis on Broadway Street.
Drivers sit on a bench outside their coaches
waiting for potential passengers to rescue them
from the bowels of boredom.

Fate fills their idle cabs with a stream of shadows.
One by one they break rank,
vanish into the vapor of distance.

When I walk out, the sun's pink eye is a dome of light.
The red-capped man and taxi drivers are ghosts.
With bill in hand, I shut the door wondering.

JUNKYARD

How we work for things
the earth will not take back—
scrape, save, borrow to possess them.

See that mountain range of old wrecked cars
with its rusted steel boulders,
crest powdered with rainbow paint ashes,
and veins of copper wire leaking through like lava?

Those mountains are worn out dreams.
Once they had shiny chrome plated smiles,
were sleek—fast, sped through time
with plumes of envy blowing out of exhaust pipes.

Now their horse power is corralled in dead engines.
Odors of decay dance like gypsies in the stiff evening air
where a river of weeds flow through barbed-wire fence.

At the highest peak, the broken windshield
of a blue 1974 Mustang with Missouri license plates
reminds me how fragile the balance of life.

Across from the base of all the wreckage,
an exiled hubcap sits in a cluster of bitterweed,
their yellow soft-toothed petals gnawing freedom.

For Mark Schiff

VI

BENEATH THE SKY

West Texas Morning

The wind smuggled cold from the north,
tucked it in its wide skirt.
In her haste to escape,
she dropped it on this desert city.

Snow collects like white words: "Warning!
I am dangerous in all of my beauty."
It mounts until lawns become soft beds
of temptation,
streets are slick with surprise
and pipes in buildings burst into cold tears.

Three days we are hostages, dressed like thieves
tiptoeing around ice.

On my way to work, the sun muscles
its way through morning.
The wet gray cowers beneath its pallid palm,
slowly withdraws itself.

An American flag flying over Music City Mall,
the water tank tattooed with *Odessa*,
and a frozen pair of black tennis shoes
appears like items on a lottery ticket.

I gamble with the air,
take off one layer of clothing
when the sky flashes a victorious smile,
then pours out heat like dreams.

For Cheryl Spears

When Last I Ate a Cantaloupe

Before I read the sign, Pecos Cantaloupes,
I saw the peak of a pile of melons.

Up close its ridged skin like a fisherman's net.
I gathered up its faceless netted head
with the finesse of a crane.

At home, I baptized it in the sink—
a ritual of caution.
I peeled into its perfumed
orange flesh with a blade,
exposing a harem of tiny seeds.

I dissected the melon like a poem.
Gutted seeds the way I do unwanted phrases,
scraped with knife its orange supple belly
until smooth, barren of seeds.

With the first bite words, like juice,
spilled into my palms.

I suckled the sweetness from my fingers,
the taste of summer sticky in my mouth.

For Earnestine, Glenda, and Lisa Walker

NAKED WINDS AND SKY

I hear "that" wail at least four aisles
over in the toy department, the one that screams
"I want" and you won't give it to me.

The wailing bolts through lights, lines, lists
and the cashier's crimson face.
She apologies for my wait, endurance
of the screaming voice, screaming as though life
severed its desires with a gator-tooth machete.

I know the weight of a wail,
a balloon lifting the voice
above pain, fear, need.
One escapes from within me,
my ears popping with emancipation.

I say to the screamer, you will live.
"No" is a priceless gift wrapped in sandpaper.
The screamer does not hear.
My words drown in silence.

I walk outside where the sun seizes sky
with chains of afternoon light, cuffs of white heat—
hear the desert scream "that" cry.
Hey, Poet! See my beauty, too!

You write of landscapes laden
with bluebells, blazing stars, azaleas.

You are delirious about the Pacific, Atlantic.
Why are their long wet tongues
more important than my dry dusty throat?

You step on my heart lusting
after fertile hills, blue mountains—green.
Look! I give you plump tumbleweeds,
cactus malls, naked winds
and sky and sky and sky.

80

For Kay Walker

To Susan Boyles

"If she doesn't get another makeover she'll be back
to the old Susan soon," the Sun quoted a source as saying. (ANI)

I walk around the neighborhood
to make the world larger,
get out of boredom's cramped room.
Dusk is a spider crawling on reeds of light.
Sprinklers continuously toss water
from their stubby black hands,
litter the sidewalks and street.

Summer is retirement age.
Temperatures are sagging
in the comfortable low seventies.
Next month it will store its green shawl,
watch fall put on crimson, amber and orange hats.

My birthday is next Sunday. There will be no fanfare.
I think about how the earth ages with splendor—
the redwoods in their crimson wisdom,
Denali in her ivory strength,
the Pacific and Atlantic in their blue courage,
and I think about you, Susan Boyles—

how you ambled on stage in your simplicity,
nervousness hidden beneath snappy words
and a hip shake.
The audience laughs because your body is not a reed,
hair not the color of morning, skin not smooth like jazz.

For Stacey Nash

BLUE PERFORMANCE

A herd, yes, a herd,
not a flock, of grackles
weighed down telephone wires,
accosted tree branches,
assaulted the city with their presence.

The raven cannibals mobbed
the air, guzzled silence,
flapped their wings,
stirred the people to anger
with their obese songs.

Anger was stirred and stirred
until it became a curtain.
Behind the curtain people plotted
and the grackles started falling
from a heated dancing sky.
Some said poison.

This afternoon on my way from work,
I found a grackle outside my door,
    fallen—its wings, great tail—motionless,
    bill pointed upwards,
    opened like an empty wallet,
    unfolding its bird language,
    singing its last accolades
to the sky's blue performance.

For Ivy Kaminsky

BLACK FEATHERS

Winter has ripped away the pecan trees' disguise
exposing every muscle and sinew,
blemish and crack,
vulnerable to the wind's strong lust for power.
It could snap its wooden tendons with one heavy sigh.

And what of our vulnerability?
How we cling to anonymity, fear transparency,
for others to see us in our humanness,
or for things old and broken to surface, spill out
from behind walls of insecurity.

Once I told a secret.
I know the blow of rejection, the crush of words,
shame rising from my countenance
like steam from an iron.

On this winter's dusk,
clouds make a gray skirt around the moon's fat bottom.
Over the pecan trees bald head,
a wave of black feathers ripples
across a rain colored sky.
The cold's icy knuckles brush my face—
batter grackles' wings, flapping, squawking
as though their out of tune melody will heat the air.

My hands are two brown rafts floating
in the warmth of my pockets when I see them—
two teenagers talking with their thumbs,
pressing buttons on cell phones,
swift, staccato, sure like the rain,
their voices drowning.

For Janette Sloper

83

THE 8TH STREET CARWASH AND DETAIL SHOP

Black Friday's two days away; today a Christmas card arrives
with this message scribbled inside:
> *The family spent the last two summers building*
> *a cabin in northern Minnesota;*
> *there is snow with the expected high of eight degrees.*

Here, heat swashes the city like summer slaver.
I take advantage of high temps,
take my Taurus to the 8th Street Carwash and Detail Shop.

There, a pierced nosed woman greets me,
takes my keys, points to a waiting room.
My car and the woman disappear
behind a worn white wall.

I sit in the small room listening
to the composition of a shoeshine rag—
slap, slap, pop; slap, slap, pop; slap, slap, pop
against a pair of black boots.

Periodically, I look out the water stained window
to make the room larger.
My eyes sweep past a mechanical waterfall,
rest on a crew of washers.
Orange flames capture my attention.
The flames spread, shoot across a Harley Davidson T-shirt.

I try to return to the waiting room, my poetry,
the slap, slap, pop medley, but I am back outside—
eyes volleying between flames and the man
with a denim shirt curled below his hips.

Veins in his bony arms resemble wires
stretched between telephone poles.
His cracked peeling hands manipulate a dingy
green towel on the hood of a white Chevy pick-up
while sweat pools beneath his arm pits, face, back—
expression colder than Minnesota's eight degrees.

84

For Carol Rudolph

UDDER BEAUTY

I watch one in animation.
Face scowled, udders dancing,
shaking like boneless fingers.
I do not remember them this way.

When I was in Vermont,
their round eyes reflected
splashes of evening's light
stained on an apron of pale amber leaves
draped over the Creamery Bridge,
its wooden shadow scraping rocks in a narrow creek.

Oh cow, you are the object of insult
but I honor you—
also the swine, hippopotamus, rhinoceros,
and what of the moose?

Even things big and gangly
belong in the delicate place of beauty
with the sumac's red wings,
the maple's fat fiery branches,
the sassafras' crushed sweet orange leaves.

The moon is growing, filling the sky
with that huge white eye.
It sees all things the same,
cows grazing, leaves changing,
a crow batting its wings against darkness,
waiting for morning's milk of light.

PINWHEEL PREDICTIONS

I am looking at New England posed in my photo album,
a white veil of fog lifting, horizon blushing
with scarlet, amber, orange

while pinwheels in my garden are squeaking,
spinning a death melody.
Their wimpy whines, woeful groans, pitiful songs
proclaim flowers are dying
and winter is crawling on the calendar.

But a fist full of butterscotch haired gaillardias,
white armed dusty millers, and begonias with rose fingers,
hang on, sing of hope, memories, wisdom—

We came from earth and will return to it
one soft petal at a time,
and morning will continue to drool on grass,
wet dead yellow blades with heavy spittle.

See how fingers of autumn air comb
through the chinaberry tree.
Last month it was a peacock—
branches feathered with fiery leaves.
Today half of it looks puny, ill with change.

When winter's cold skin covers it,
that tree will become a skeleton—
pale limbs suspended in gray air,
and you will walk on its fallen dead leaves,
forgetting about their former glory.

WEEPING

Photo, "Loneliness Weeps"
by Mary Schaefer

Loneliness weeps
like spring's first hard rain.
Cries until the maple's green lashes
are crimson curled burdens.
How heavy are burdens.

The maple with its hundred strong arms
cannot hold them.
They fall beside its long thick leg.
Spread like chickenpox,
cover the shoulders of a deserted road.

They are witnesses, testaments
that the smallest of things can grow beyond holding.
Even the fog in its gray parka cannot conceal this truth.
What name shall we give these things? Fear? Loss? Grief?

Beyond all burdens
a lone leaf hangs on a limber twig.
Even in isolation, it offers faith.

See the tear drooping down its brown streaked face
and the hole where fate bit through?
On the other side, is light dancing.

For Karen Hembree

REFLECTION

Go ahead, give me that compliment
swimming in your mouth.
This ego can fit inside my vocabulary.

If I knew every word to describe life,
then I would be as Narcissus,
longing for himself in a pool of water,
spurning all suitors soliciting his love.

Had he stepped into the pool,
let the water wash him in humility,
he would have known true beauty—

koi in her red kimono,
mandarinfish in her imperial robe,
moving about in their wet kingdom,
clueless of their loveliness.

With eyes fixed on his own face,
he knew only loneliness' embrace.
What sadness to drown in self.

How grateful I am to know only this of life:
it is an ocean of forgiveness.
The moment it dries like a desert, we'll lose sight
of gifts buried beneath the most offensive
and forget why we loved the dead.

AGING SPRING

Spring is nearing middle age.
There are patches of bald spots still
throughout the city,
but the grass in this lawn is thick
with green, feels like a hard mattress.

The sun lashes my back with its hot hand
as though reprimanding me for working
in this coo of weeds,
for leaving tiny wounds in the earth,
for not thinking of you more often.

But I thought of you today,
with sweat bleeding through my blouse,
memories wedged in my back pocket
between soiled gloves and dirt.

How can something that feels so harsh
be healing?
Sun, soil, memories
of you being lowered in the ground.
There are no metaphors for that wintry November day.

I wound the earth once more, this time with a spade,
plant mature begonias, scatter marigold and zinnia seeds
like ashes.
They will grow— rainbow heads thick as calliflour.
My thumbs will puff with pride
when my neighbors say, "How beautiful!"

How beautiful was your life,
the way you found joy
in a chili dog, hope
in a broken bird's wing, light
in a stone.

In Memory of Linda Stevenson Butler

VII

CAFETERIA CONVERSATIONS

LESSONS FROM TREES

If you ask,
students will say my skin is made of music,
the grackle would say obsession.
But to know me, ask the naked limbs of oak
in Comfort, Texas.

They look like dendrites in our brains.
Look how they have grown together, depend on each other.

If they can mimic minds, they can keep secrets.
With my tongue still as the sleeping wind,
I tell them what is hidden in my sock.
It is a place where I only allow God to go
but not often.

Things I do not want
to repeat or reveal are hidden there.
My silence makes them
like the apricot, peach and plum,
soft flesh protecting seeds in hard stony shells.

With my head tilted like a telescope,
I stare at a forest of stars
while my bunched sock rubs discomfort
against my heel.
If I remove my shoe, everything I have concealed
will spill out, and I can only handle freedom
one cracked seed at a time.

For Pam Hicks

SHADOWS

Poetry is the only art people haven't yet learned to consume like soup.
—W. H. Auden

I want to slip acceptance into a bowl
of Campbell's Alphabet Soup.
Maybe she will swallow it then,
give up this fixation
with bony bare shouldered teens
displayed on glossy pages of deceit.

Seduction is too large
for their thin young frames,
but some photographer stretched
their pubescent smiles.

How can I tell a modest girl
who writes poetry and plays Bach
she is beautiful, when she can only hear
pimples complaining on her face?

And how can I convince a man
who walks in the shadow
of his brother's wealth he is valuable?
That his dirty honest hands,
sweaty blue collar uniform,
and steel-toed boots
helped build gold dreams?

How can I mold a dream,
use images like a scaffold,
snag strong verbs from the deep throat
of a full sentence, make them desirable
as the white stone of acquittal?

BOUNTY

Fear is bountiful as corn,
certainty fragile as drifting brown leaves.
This morning's headlines read like an obituary
for our nation. I will not use this space
to repeat the despondency.

I fold the paper, look outside and wish
the writers would do the same,
at least for this day.
How wonderful it is.

The sun is alive with light,
trees smile with gold and crimson teeth,
the air feels like a cup of warm coco,
and the sky's blue face is smudged
with small patches of white.

Grass on the school playground
has such delight for children's happy feet
and full throated giggles
it clings, trails them into the building.

Thanksgiving is next week.
In my music class, students sing
of the things they are thankful for:
family, friends, food,
country, shelter, pets and God.

What a harvest of joy they are.
Their voices are tender with wonder
when they ask, "What are you thankful for?"
I tell them, "Each of you."
The room radiates with embarrassing smiles,
but their eyes are flares of approval.

For Becky Morris

When children speak, listen.
There are treasures in the syntax of their innocence.

WEST TEXAS WINTER

The moon is knocking at my door.
—Faith

The sun kept surveillance
over the city for hours.
From the porch, I watched
its tired eye struggle to remain open.
A cache of crimson and pink
sagged like folds of skin
falling across a basset hound's face.

Valiant shafts of fading light wrestled free,
bled through the chinaberry's orange Mohawk leaves.
Soon a bitter cold front
will shave the rest of the tree's leafy head.
What will hide its chubby branches,
the hungry squirrel,
and the sky's evening bruised cheeks'
vast dusky smile?

See how it laughs at day and night
sparring for a position in this corner of the earth.
It knows who will wear the victor's mantle
at this hour's end.

Standing in Mama "E's" peace,
with the wind wrapped around my shoulders,
I listen to car tires slap against the street,
my neighbor's muted conversations
and think how pure is this season
in its kindness, cruelty, bare beauty,
its immodest, unpretentious self.

A wind chime's sudden whisper
shakes me from stillness.
With the moon knocking at my door
and winter tapping on my back,
I walk inside where scents of pumpkin
burn from a candle's open mouth
and darkness dusts the day from my shoes.

PIZZA

Jason

His seven year-old body spasms with impatience
as he waits for the lunch line to move forward.
"Jason," I get his attention using my most teacherly voice.
He turns, faces me with a warm smile,
plastic spork in one hand, the other directing air.

"Give me some of your energy; this old lady needs some."
You're not old, he reprimands.

"When you're my age, I will be ninety-five
and I will probably still be here.
Will you come back to see me?" I say.

Miss Walker, I can't come back to see you.
I am going to be a fireman; I will be at work.

My dear child, I want to say, the distance
between tomorrow and "the future" is the same;
both are filled with opaque miles of uncertainty,
but possibility is wrapped around their broad shoulders.
Hug them like brothers.

You breathe in now with confidence, your speech staccato,
rapid as you tell me what you plan to do.
I listen to your dreams while you exhale the past,
your voice a siren flashing promise.

For my PBG's—Melanie Key, Julie Sorum and Debbie Hensley

Wandering Happiness

Joel

My happiness is gone on vacation,
he says, eyes dribbling with sadness—
six-year old shoulders hunched in defeat.

"Where did happiness go?" I ask.
Traveling on a turtle's back?
In a shiny ceramic sea shell,
or cheese on an overstuffed taco?

He tells me, head sandwiched
between his hands,
I don't know. It just left my brain.

Maybe the sky lifted it,
hid it in an eagle's agile wings,
or tucked it away in a kangaroo's bib.

Maybe it's sitting alone?
Rooting in Oahu's sandy mouth
drenched in colors
of African tulips, plumerias, day lilies.

Maybe it's watching white sails
dot the ocean like ellipses,
or listening to soft swirls roll
from the Pacific's long tongue
as day drifts into a pink comatose sky.

"I bet we can get it back," I say.
His chin quivers with hope.
Do you think we can get it back by Friday?

How I wish my smiling heart was contagious.
However, I must leave him quarantined
in the unhappiness of himself, knowing
joy is leaping from the pages of the next song.

For Nancy Clark

KOLACHE

Amanda

Her smile is a scalpel
cutting away the gloom
of Monday morning.

Sleepy, I eat a kolache
swathed in mustard.

Before finishing this impromptu breakfast,
I hear, *Surprise!*
Her thick wavy hair is at least a ruler long,
eyes alert like an owl,
face the shape of a small dinner plate.

"What a wonderful surprise you are,"
I say while wiping away crumbs.
My mother calls me mi cielo.

You are your mother's heaven
and my reminder of how beautiful the sky,
and the way I saw it this morning
before children started piling into the building
with their books and opportunities.

The moon was still a perfect circle.
I marveled at the morning light
and music swarming around the moon.
It was the "o" in how lovely.

Now, as I walk into dusk gazing at mi cielo
the pond in Memorial Garden Park lures the sun
the way you lured me into the beauty of your smile.

With its golden head dipping slowly,
I watch it disappear into the depth
of the pond's dark wet lair.

mi cielo . . . my heaven

CHEESE SANDWICH

Donovan

Two limp dollar bills sag between my fingers
as I struggle with the lid on a thermos
of chicken noodle soup.

His fingers are like pliers pulling
the crust from two slices of white bread.
My eyes are question marks.
I like to eat the crusty part by itself,
he explains while unwrapping a slice of cheese.

He hikes glasses higher on his nose,
crafts his sandwich with the patience of a monk.
When he bites, mayonnaise makes tiny white clouds
around his six-year old smile.

He says my name with such mischief
I think mischief is my name.
With the curls on his head spiraling like broken bed springs,
he demands, *Let me have that money in your hand.*

"This is my lunch money."
He debates. That's not enough to buy your lunch.
I rally, "You don't know how much I have."

His voice is strong with conviction,
You have two dollars and two dollars
equal eight quarters or four stickers.

How elegant the math of boldness,
dividing need and want with the wit of innocence.

For Alice Deras

MASHED POTATOES

Caleb

Balancing a lunch tray like an acrobat,
he walks like a branch burdened
with too many peaches.

His sandy blonde hair is spiked like cactus,
faded blue eyes busy while he licks
mashed potatoes and gravy from his thumb.

My shadow must have been his cue.
When he sees me, he holds his stomach
as though pain is made of flesh.

There is too much joy
around the corners of his mouth
for distress.

He calls to me, face exaggerated with urgency.
Miss Walker, when I laugh, my stomach hurts!
"Aah, that's what you call a belly laugh.
It means your soul is happy."

It hurts for my soul to be happy.

How I wish I could make him understand
joy brought by pain—his birth,
a burning heart before a gold medal,
truth in all of its complexities.

He is nine, knows only what's immediate.
When he lives beyond half a century
and gray creeps around the edges of his face,
he will comprehend.

For now, I say, "You'll be okay."
I pat him on his willowy shoulder, walk away,
taking his warmth with me to the next child in need.

For Barbara Browning

AT MEMORIAL GARDEN PARK

Carlos

As darkness roams in the October evening sky,
I watch the light from an airplane blink
into the distance, get lost among the few stars
sagging beneath the moon's bottom lip.

A white throated falcon perches
on a telephone wire, chest puffed like a demi-god,
a motley chorus of dogs pant with joy
after squeeze toys,
Canadian geese shuffle
from water to grass snatching
at cracker crumbs.

Routine has sapped my creativity,
made me frugal with my imagination.
I concentrate on ducks paddling across the pond,
creating perfect wet "v's."

Although my body is pulsating with fatigue,
I chase my shadow for three miles,
trying to empty my mind of the day.
But it wanders back to class.

We are singing "Old McDonald."
After the cow sound, your eyes are glazed
with revelation, cheeks puffed like the falcon's chest.
Miss Walker, when you pull the cow's stomach
to get milk, it goes moo-ooo.

As when you tug at my heart
with your five year-old wisdom,
I swallow the resistance of hurting your feelings,
choking on my laughter.

For Michele Allen

102

Spicy Pumpkin

McKenzie

Her swift movement makes a lightning blink
look like a snail's crawl.
She wraps her arms around my waist
the way heat does the sun,
hugging as though squeezing a tube of toothpaste.

She flashes a smile, buries her six year-old head
in my blouse. With another quick motion,
she looks up at me and says,
Miss Walker, you don't smell like you.

Usually I smell of Juniper Breeze
but this morning I am fall scented—Sweet Spicy Pumpkin.
Her words, the scent of my skin
send me walking through my own memory.

I am in Vermont with friends
driving through fall's bazaar of beauty,
looking at leaves sing an October medley
of orange, pink, and amber—
the Wallomsac River mimicking
with a watery smile.

Red echoes across the horizon,
bouncing from Mount Mansfield
to Killington Peak.
Earth's crimson voice shouting,
"Look at me. I am lovely, aren't I?"

We rummage through our vocabulary
searching for words, hear ourselves cutting air
with sharp deep breaths.
When words find our tongues, they are primitive.

We say, "Oh, my! Look at that!"

How beautiful are those memories—
the earth disrobing in purity, revealing beauty secrets
before taking a cold nap. How wonderful is this moment,
your small arms extended, offered as tokens of trust.

For Sharla Butler

EYES FORWARD

Emma

Morning is tired and sagging,
waiting for noon.
In fifteen minutes, it will rest
until tomorrow.
In fifteen minutes, a fresh batch of faces
will stir in the school's cafeteria
where the aroma of pepperoni pizza
seeps in the skin.

I watch children enter in a crooked line,
dragging hunger with them.
Emma watches, too.
Her six-year old smile is a beacon
of delight and pale blue eyes are like a telescope
focused in the distance.
Miss Walker, you know that boy Keatyn in fourth grade?
He's my future boyfriend.

Words cannot swim their way out through the stream
of laughter flowing in my stomach.
I cast my gaze like a net in the direction
of her intended catch.

His nine year old face is kind,
riddled with early signs of handsomeness,
clueless hands stained with pizza sauce.

He eats his lunch with the vigor of a warrior,
but he is prey, caught in the trap
of a huntress who can barely tie her shoes.

For Lynn Gawlik

LUNCH PROPOSAL

Madison

Humility is limp,
impotent as blanks in a musket
when she shoots to her seven year old feet.

Her sky faded eyes are softer than candlelight,
but there is no timidity
in her Mars colored cheeks.

She abandons her lunch, flattens her hands
on the table and does not leave room
for race or age, gender or station when she asks,
Miss Walker, will you marry me?

I've eaten more laughter than tears
after teaching twenty-eight years.
I take another bite of it,
disguise what I am chewing.
"No, I can't marry you. I am too old."

Seven years have made her determination
strong like the Golden Gate's crimson legs.
We can work this out and have a baby name Bob.

How I wish we could work things out—
war, famine, poverty, differences.
Hate, harsh words, and cruelty
would fizzle like Alka-Seltzer.

We cannot put these dark things in a glass,
pour them in the Mississippi's muddy shoes.
Nor can I be her wife.

She sees only the simplicity of love.
I will take her light, lock it in the cabinet
next to my desk and leave the key dangling
for the world to grab hold.

For Michelle Norrid

106

INQUISITION

Jelisha

Winter is past its prime.
Sniffles of spring infect the air.

My stomach is singing louder than I am—
a requiem of hunger.
Dinner is in grave clothes. Breakfast eludes me.
I am left with longing.

It's an hour before lunch when a curious
first grader converts my classroom
into a stage of inquisition.

Her voice is small, probing.
"Miss Walker, do you have a Mama?"
"Yes, I do."
A chorus of six year-old voices echoes
throughout the room, "Everybody got a Mama."

"What's her name?"
"Mary."
My answer is like a conductor's baton.
From different sections of the room I hear,
"My mother's name is Mary."
"My grandmother's name is Mary."

Questions fill her eyes, blind them
like closed shutters.
My skin is the color of night.
Still she asks, *"Is she black?"*
"Yes, she is."
She is relentless with her interview,
determination stronger than a bear trap.
"Do you have a father?"

107

"Yes, I do."
"What's his name?"
"Robert."

"Do you have a husband?"
"No, I don't."
"I gotta hook you up then."

When you hook me up,
connect my limbs to love's green vines.
Bind my hands with soft cords of passion,
then leave me singing in winter's aging joy.

For Barbara Nay

A very dear friend asked Loretta, "When are you going to write a novel and make some real money? You have some great ideas." Her answer for now is this. Novelists take ideas and create stories. Poets take a word and create a universe. If one is blessed to be both, what a gift they are to the world. One day she hopes to write a novel. But today she is a poet and music teacher at Reagan Elementary in Odessa, Texas. She graduated from Ector High School, received a Bachelor of Music Education degree from Texas Tech University and earned a Master's of Elementary Education from the University of Texas at the Permian Basin. Loretta is active in her community through membership in organizations such as Texas Music Educators Association, Delta Sigma Theta Sorority, Inc. and the Permian Basin Poetry Society. She is also a member of the Poetry Society of Texas, the Pennsylvania Poetry Society, the Poetry Society of Oklahoma, Abilene Writer's Guild, the National Federation of Poetry Societies, and the Texas Mountain Trail Writers.

Loretta believes kindness is a language in and of itself, she hopes to speak it fluently. She also believes when children speak, listen. There are treasures in the syntax of their innocence.

Printed in the United States of America

www.ingramcontent.com/pod-product-compliance
Lightning Source LLC
Chambersburg PA
CBHW031858090426
42741CB00005B/542

Loretta Walker's *Word Ghetto* is a rich multi-dimensional kaleidoscope of Life, turning your mind and senses like the Milky Way galaxy, while freeing your heart to embrace your Oneness. Who would have thought Kali, the Black Goddess, was living in West Texas disguised as Loretta Walker? And like Kali, Loretta Walker crushes your separateness with her enchanting dance of Life through the *Word Ghetto*. Read it and be free.

—George E. James, Author of *Peeling the Onion: Poems of Spiritual Awakening* and *Copperhead: Tantric Lessons on Love.*

Loretta Diane Walker writes with compassionate wisdom and insight—her poems restore humanity.

—Naomi Shihab Nye

Loretta Walker's Word Ghetto is an astounding book, full of wisdom, compassion, and masterfully woven word magic. Her language speaks with a rich tapestry of emotion, and her poems sing like a saxophone playing the music of her soul. Loretta Walker's vision is huge – she speaks for a whole community of people who are marginalized by the circumstances of their birth. Her poems offer healing, vision and hope."

—Diane Frank, Author of *Blackberries in the Dream House* and *Entering the Word Temple*

In this accomplished book, Loretta Diane Walker, poet, musician and teacher, draws us into her word music, and convinces us to inhabit her deepest concerns—children, race in America, pain and forgiveness, the changing body, the open soul—to revel in language and life with her, to wonder and to grieve. Walker finds beauty so thoroughly entrenched in the quotidian, we are glad to enter her world, even though it is not untarnished. Her fierce poems temper hope with honesty, conviction with clarity of vision. Startlingly fresh without posturing or distraction, they pull us from whatever routine threatens to dull our senses. From the tenderness of the teacher to her young students, through memories of her childhood, and her involvement in the lived experiences of others, she holds a mirror to the revelations of a grounded life.

—Mary Kay Rummel, Author of *What's Left is the Singing*

. . . connect my limbs to love's green vines.
Bind my hands with soft cords of passion,
then leave me singing in winter's aging joy.

(Inquisition)

It (poetry) lives.
I saw its round belly protruding
through my neighbor's red blouse.
She thinks it is a boy, but it is poetry.

(Poetry's Assassination)